# LIVING
# BEYOND
## *the*
# MEMORY

FINDING *HOPE* AND *HEALING*
THROUGH GRIEF

# CHERIE JOBE

# Dedication

*To those who are living in a world of "withouts." The world without enough tears to fill the hollowness of your soul. The world with no response to the whispers of their absence. This books is dedicated to you!*

# Contents

# A Note From The Author

You are never prepared for the death of a loved one, whether it comes slowly or suddenly and unexpected. No matter the situation, you face many painful questions. It is my greatest hope that we can answer some of those for you through the pages of this book.

Two things in life change you, and you are never the same:

Love and Grief.

# Introduction

If you have picked up this book, chances are you have, or someone dear to you has lost a loved one.

This is a book that I never thought, in a million years, I would write. We all are aware that death and taxes are things that will invade our lives at some point along our journey. Despite that knowledge, the loss of a partner, child, parent, or just someone you love dearly creates a Grand Canyon size hole in your heart. The impact brought by it dramatically changes your present and your future.

I'm forever thankful for my husband, Jim, who for 16 years was such a part of my existence. Just knowing and loving him made me such a better wife, mother, "Mimi," and friend. I'd love to tell you a bit about him.

He was called "Jimmy" by those who lived in his hometown. I chose to call him Jim, or "Baby Love" when I needed some honey-dos done.

His life reflected the qualities we are taught in Colossians 3:12: *compassion, kindness, humility, gentleness, and patience.* Jim was a man of great character, who genuinely loved his fellow man, but also could defend his values and fight till the end for those he loved.

Beginning at a young age, Jim loved fishing, hunting, and cars. What most people never knew was that he was a gifted artist. He never shared that talent much because, like most artists, he never thought he was good enough.

He always told me the most rewarding job throughout his job career was when he was the director of the Tennessee Vocational School.

He felt so much at home, helping young men and women with their future careers.

Jim and I first met on "Friend Day" at a local church in my little hometown. His daughter and son-in-law introduced us. Since Jim was recently divorced and I was the singles group leader, I thought just maybe I could connect him with our gathering, called Circle of Friends.

Circle of Friends would meet on Tuesday night potluck, and I remember just like it was yesterday. The doors swung open, and in walked this handsome, gray-headed guy carrying a bucket of fried chicken. He was wearing a white button-down collared shirt, starched khaki slacks, and sported the most beautiful smile that immediately had all the ladies' heads turning.

Jim captured my heart, even before I realized it, and six months later, on March 30, 2002, I became Mrs. James N. Jobe Sr. We both knew that God's plan had brought us together. Jim was 60, and I was 45, but numbers were never an issue for us because our love for each other far outweighed the odds of who would leave this life first.

Jim and I both brought into our marriage two grown daughters and two grown sons.

Jim's life was also characterized by a heart of service and love and care for others. On the one hand, he was known as being quiet and reserved when in a group but became very personable and caring when speaking to people one-on-one. Someone told me one time that when Jim spoke, everyone listened because they knew it would always be something that would bring wisdom to the conversation.

I believe the best word to describe Jim is "a man of character." He was a man you could trust to do what he said he would do. He was a true southern gentleman. Jim completed me and I always felt safe in his arms.

He was always ready to lend a hand or dig in to help those in need. He delighted in the simple pleasures and events of life but also had an adventurous side. He adored his five grandchildren, who, in turn, adored him.

His love for Jesus Christ, his personal Savior, radiated in everything he did. Jim was always smiling and had some encouraging words to say to those in his path.

When I think of Jim's entry to his new home in heaven, I believe he heard his Father say, "Well done, my faithful servant."

> Jim, I'm so looking forward to one day seeing you again, my love.
>
> —Cherie

Believe me. It's hard to walk through this thing called grief. It's not a one and done thing, just so you know. Much like writing this book, It's a process!

Right now, though, it is the time to feel the pain and all the emotions that go with it. Don't allow others to tell you how you should feel. Please be patient with yourself, and don't judge your pain with someone else's pain.

Talk about your loss and memories to someone you can trust. Remember, Rome wasn't built in a day, and neither will your new life be, so hang in there with me as we travel this road together.

## Chapter 1

# A Turbulent Future

"I Love You."

Three words, that's all. Those three words are the beginning of a relationship are ones most people believe will last a lifetime. I had searched all my life for true love, for my soul mate, my knight in shining armor, and now that I had it, I felt so thankful and blessed.

### DISRUPTION

My life, as I knew it, changed forever on June 3, 2016. I had been with my daughter on a business trip to Knoxville. On our way down, I mentioned to her that Jim wasn't talking much to me, and I was concerned he was upset with me over something.

Jim and I had this policy of talking through our differences, even if we had really disagreed on something. So, I told my daughter I'm not sure what's up with him. Is he so mad at me that he's decided to break our policy of talking it out?

We were to be in Knoxville for three days but decided to come home a day early. I spent most of the time away thinking about how I was going to get to the bottom of Jim's quietness. He had *never* been angry with me to the point of not speaking for days. I had my guns drawn, ready to defend myself at whatever the accusations he was about to make.

Having been away for two days, I was so excited to see him, even though I knew a confrontation was coming. We immediately embraced as I walked through the door since we were not apart very much. Unlike a lot of couples, we really enjoyed being together.

I put my things away and proceeded to sit in the family room to talk about my trip, totally ignoring for a moment the BIG PINK ELEPHANT in the room.

Immediately, out of Jim's mouth came the three words I needed so much to hear from him, "I Love You."

OK, I thought now is the time (because timing is everything in a discussion) to address the BIG PINK ELEPHANT in the room.

I remember saying, "I love you too, but something is wrong." He looked me straight in the eyes, and with all the strength he had, he muttered," I can't seem to get my words out. Immediately, I thought he had a stroke or a mini-stroke.

OMG, now what do I do? Do I take him to the hospital? What? OMG, I wish now he had been mad at me instead of this.

In Jim's mind, he knew he already had a doctor's appointment on Monday, so he thought if he could just keep quiet and make it till Monday, he wouldn't have to make a visit to the ER. Well, that sounds like the thinking of most men!

He knew me well, too, and with much persuasion from his children and his medical doctor, that's exactly where we had him the next morning. The hospital ran all kinds of tests, and, thankfully, all the tests showed it was not a stroke. So, what in the world is it, I asked?

Their response was, "We are not sure, but we want him to see a neurologist."

Trying to get an appointment with a neurologist without the help of your regular doctor and God is like watching wet paint dry on the wall—it takes FOREVER!

Even so, we began to jump through hoops trying to get an appointment with the best neurologist in Nashville. We gathered names, and with the good Lord's help, were able to get an appointment with one of the top neurologists in Nashville.

So the journey begins!

## MY JOURNAL

### My Journal: August 9, 2016

*Today is the day that my life, as I have known it, changed. It started off with an appointment with the neurologist in Nashville at 10:30 am. Jim's daughter asked if she could come to the appointment. We were fine with it because it puts another set of eyes and ears to the conversation. It was nice to have his daughter drive so Jim and I could just sit back and relax. I felt a little stress coming from Jim. I'm sure he was wondering what the doctor would say. That small little room began to feel even smaller as we all sat anxiously waiting for the doctor's entrance.*

*Suddenly, entered a very tall, lanky gentleman with not much bedside manners, who immediately got right to the point.*

*He proceeded to say, "Jim, you are a strong and fit man. Your bloodwork and all your tests look fine. I don't believe you have had a stroke or a mini-stroke. You have a 'degenerative brain disease.' You also have aphasia, which is a symptom of this brain disease."*

*OMG, we are all in shock!*

*His instructions were to start speech therapy and get a PET scan, so we can get a better look at this disease and where it's located.*

*My heart is broken and hurting for Jim. I remember those words in our wedding vows, "For sickness and in health." We are battling this disease together!*

He heals the brokenhearted and binds up their wounds: Psalms 147:3

CHAPTER 2

# Playing the Waiting Game

Having to sit and listen to a doctor tell someone you love dearly that he potentially has a brain disease is terrifying. Everything about that conversation vividly stands out to me. It's as though somebody hit a "freeze" button and the movie of our life stopped at that instant.

With that backdrop, we began the journey of speech therapy, MRIs, Cat Scans, Pet Scans, and fights with the insurance companies.

I remember vividly when Jim met with his new speech therapist. She tried to explain how the muscles in the mouth and throats are used for speech, chewing, and swallowing. Using some new technologies, they were hoping to improve Jim's speech issues. I was so thankful that we weren't having any swallowing issues. Jim knew exactly what he wanted to say; he just couldn't make it come out as fluently as usual. The therapist asked me to keep a daily evaluation of Jim's speech, thinking, and tiredness, and that is when I started the journal.

**MY JOURNAL: AUGUST 10, 2016**

*I asked Jim if he had done his speech homework today and he said he had to get the yard mowed. Sounded so much like a typical man—first things first. He did speech around lunch then again at 4:00 pm. I noticed that after mowing and doing speech exercises, by 6:00 pm, he could hardly speak.*

*Evaluation for the Day:*
*1-10 1 being bad/10 good*
*Speech-4*
*Tiredness-4*
*Thinking-9*

Have you ever hurt so badly that you couldn't breathe? Hurt so bad you're not able to even speak. You walk around in a daze, not remembering what you just did or even ate. You can't sleep. You even attempt to act normal, so people don't realize you're not OK.

It's sometimes so bad that you even ask questions like, "God, why is this happening? What did we do to deserve this? God, do you even care?"

We are never prepared for the death of a loved one, whether it comes sudden or unexpected. Some of the emotions that travel alongside us are sadness, heartache, and emptiness. As you travel this road, there will be many questions like, "Will I ever find peace and joy again?" One thing we must do in the beginning is to accept and embrace our feelings. Whatever those are, it's OK to feel like that. We cannot heal what we cannot feel!

We also have to let people know what we need. Family and friends so want to help but just don't know what to do. I felt scared that our family might feel like I wasn't doing my job as Jim's caretaker, even though it was killing me. That was purely my self-doubt, not anyone judging me. The truth is, you have to tell someone you need a physical and emotional break. Just know it's NOT a reflection on you; it's for your survival!

### My Journal: August 11, 2016

*Today has been very emotional for both Jim and me. Not sure why; maybe we need to purge all the emotions bottled up inside. Tears have flowed freely today.*

*Our pastor came and anointed and prayed that the disease stays contained.*

*Evaluation for the Day:*
*Speech-7*
*Tiredness-8*
*Thinking-8*
*Good Day!*

## MY JOURNAL: AUGUST 16, 2016

*We had a date night at The Grand Ole Opry with our friends Rob and Shearon Clifton to see Darius Rucker. We had a blast! Sometimes laughter takes your mind off the stresses of life.*
    *Pet Scan scheduled for next Thursday at 10:30 am. We got word today we are going to Alaska in September for my 60th birthday!*

*Evaluation for the Day*
*Speech-6*
*Tiredness-5*
*Thinking-10*

## MY JOURNAL: AUGUST 27, 2016

*Jim seems to be having a good day. Speech is really slow but clear. I bought Jim and me rain boots for our Alaska trip. We are so excited as Alaska has always been on our bucket list.*

*Evaluation for the Day:*
*Speech-8*
*Tiredness-7*
*Thinking-7*

*We got a call from the neurologist today. We believe it's good news and a sign that God is working. He said his cat scan looked good with no frontal lobe dementia. There was a possibility that because of some family history, there just might be some evidence. We are continuing to pray for healing.*

> *Evaluation of the Day:*
> *Speech-8*
> *Tiredness-7*
> *Thinking-8*

As I walked through this challenging time, many of my daily thoughts and actions were to try to keep things as normal as possible. To respect Jim's manhood and his wishes to continue his life for as long as possible.

I'm betting you right now you're wondering, so what do I do with all the uncertainties of this disease?

Coming from the caretaker's side, I just wanted to fix *everything* for him. That's just what we do! He wasn't one who allowed me to do many things for him. He was a very independent man.

Because of that, I talked to God, asking what my place was as his wife? I loved him more than life itself, but the truth was, this was his life, and I had to accept his rules. Sometimes all we can do is wait for answers from God.

## My Journal: September 5, 2016

*Labor Day-Jim, of course, continues to labor! That's just who he is. He worked at church all day yesterday and painted today. I'm having a hard time getting him to rest. I do understand he so wants to be productive, but we are continuing to monitor his speech, and are finding it is being altered by his tiredness that work brings on.*

*Evaluation of the Day:*
*Speech-6*
*Tiredness-6*
*Thinking-7*


## MY JOURNAL: SEPTEMBER 17-24ᵀᴴ, 2016

*Celebrating my 60ᵗʰ birthday on an Alaskan cruise—a thrill of a lifetime! Never could possibly imagine the beauty of Alaska. So thankful we are able to experience this breathtaking experience together. Jim is having a blast but gets so tired by the end of the day.*


## MY JOURNAL: OCTOBER 6, 2016

*Starting to really see Jim's speech decline. Really getting hard for me to understand him. It's making him really frustrated with me.*

As a child, I was taught not to express feelings of emotions because it would show a sign of weakness. I know you might be feeling a bit frustrated right now. Here are a few suggestions that helped me when I felt helpless seeing Jim decline:

- Talking with someone you trust, not texting. It may help you be clearer about what you are feeling.
- Write your feelings in a journal. It helps to see the list that's bothering you.
- Remind yourself that there are things that are just beyond your control.

## My Journal: October 11, 2016

*My 60ᵗʰ birthday is today and I'm sitting in Vanderbilt's ER. Jim is not doing well today. The doctors had to have him admitted to hopefully see what's going on. I'm very happy with the care he's getting.*

*Sweet nurse brought me a birthday balloon today, and little did I know, some friends had planned a 60ᵗʰ surprise birthday party for me. Oh well, they just froze my cake to eat at a later time.*


## My Journal: October 24, 2016

*Things Jim can no longer do, or having major trouble with:*

- *Stand on one leg to put slacks on*
- *Losing major muscle mass*
- *Able to do much handwriting*

*We got Jim an appointment at Cleveland Clinic. Whatever this is, it seems to be getting much worse. Beginning to scare me to death, just not knowing what to do.*


## My Journal: November 2, 2016

*I flew to Cleveland today and almost didn't find a room as people were everywhere. We learned later the World Series was in town. Cubs take the win!*

*This huge hospital is amazing. I knew my way around a bit, because my brother-in-law had his lung transplant there.*

Let's talk a bit about trying to balance living life and dealing with someone ill. Should we feel bad about trying to live a somewhat normal life?

Absolutely not!!!!! Knowledge is power!

We must have some sense of normalcy, or you will go absolutely nuts. Taking care of someone sick weakens even the most resilient. If you are a caregiver, take steps to preserve your own health and well-being. Here are a few tips for keeping you healthy:

- 7-9 hours of sleep each night
- Eat a healthy diet
- Get at least 30 minutes of walking
- Get your yearly physical

LOVING YOURSELF enough to take care of you is so important at this time.

### MY JOURNAL: NOVEMBER 3, 2016

*Put Jim through extensive testing today. The doctors at Cleveland Clinic didn't agree with the diagnosis of Vanderbilt hospital. The doctor's response was unexpected. His words were said with confidence: "I believe you have a Motor Neuron Disease, much like ALS." It was all I could do not to fall to the floor screaming, "NO! Not ALS." Jim and I went back to our room in disbelief. Jim is in shock, and my heart is absolutely broken. Much like ALS, the doctor said, "Well, is it, or isn't it." That's the million-dollar question at this time.*

### MY JOURNAL: NOVEMBER 4, 2016

*Jim started tests at 7:15 this morning. He is handling this so well, outwardly, but on the inside, he and I are so scared right now.*

*My friend Karen gave me this little book that asks questions like "What's going to happen now?" "Do I have the strength to get through this?" This verse reminds me where my strength comes from: Psalms 4:8 "In peace I will lie down and sleep, for you alone, Lord make me dwell in safety."*

Most of us aren't prepared for bad news, and it's a learned process to figure out what comes next. One of the most important things I have learned is you can't do this all by yourself. I really do know this because I tried to carry the load all by myself. You must reach out to family and friends for support.

## MY JOURNAL: NOVEMBER 10, 2016

*We are to fly out this morning. Still not having our questions answered a hundred percent but trusting Our God to comfort us during this time of uncertainty.*

## MY JOURNAL: NOVEMBER 13-19, 2016

*Left to spend a week with the Cliftons at the beach and the weather was fabulous! Good friends are priceless. It is really good to take our minds off of all this for a short period of time. Jim loves to lay out in the sun. He gets the most amazing tan. He's so handsome with his little brown body and beautiful white teeth. Learning to appreciate every moment we have together as if it's our last.*

Friends are a constant reminder of God's blessings. True friendship cannot be bought or sold. Its value is far greater than a mountain of gold.

7 Traits of a good friend: honest, low maintenance, non-judgmental, loyal, respectful of your thoughts, and trustworthy

Life is a Gift—spend it with a friend!

## MY JOURNAL: DECEMBER 4, 2016

*Today we leave for Mayo Clinic in Rochester. Still trying to find out answers. It has been a hard trip for Jim. He has had 2-3 appointments a day for a week. When we arrived, they had their first snowfall, which wasn't much, but when we left, they had 8 inches on the ground. It is SO cold here, like 15 below* zero. *The diagnosis that was given after days of testing, was an "Upper Motor Neuron Disease," that will most likely go into ALS. There's that wicked word again, that scares me to death. I'm trying so hard to not cry, but today when I heard this diagnosis, I walked out of the room while Jim was dressing and literally fell apart. I thought I was going to die. I couldn't breathe. I had to call my good friend and try to explain through all my tears what the diagnosis was. I had a complete breakdown for a few minutes, then had to pull myself together and be strong for Jim.*

*The doctors said if there's any good news it's that's it's not in the lower part of the brain. Our prayer is that it's slow-acting, with slow progression.*

I know God hears every word that's uttered from our mouths. Believe it or not, there are blessings that come from seasons of desperation. Desperation was exactly the season we were in. So many prayers that God would answer was a victory. Slowing down this terrible disease is a victory we would take!

### My Journal: December 23-30, 2016

*I'm so sick with strep throat! Yuck. We had to call off all Christmas events.*

### My Journal: January 1, 2017

*Happy New Year! Still have two days of antibiotics left-feeling much better. Trying to stay away from Jim, so he won't get this crud! My favorite verse I cling to is Jerimiah 29:11 "I know the plans I have for you, Cherie!"*

### My Journal: January 10, 2017

*My whole life has been consumed by caretaking my sweet husband. I so wish I could fix this disease. That's what I'm good at, fixing problems! I'm crying a lot right now, just out of frustration and the possibility I'm losing the love of my life.*

Finding a balance in caretaking is crucial. When we balance our caretaking, we become a better spouse and friend. Consider maybe two days a week you could possibly hire a paid caregiver to come in while you do something for yourself. Maybe just take a walk, do some sort of exercise, meet a friend for lunch, or go shopping. I found if I don't take care of myself this way, I become short-tempered, frustrated, anxious, and exhausted.

When a crisis hits, it changes everything. Often, we lose our identity, and we might have to lose our jobs, or push our friends to the backburner. Even though this sometimes can't be helped, we must begin to put some normalcy back in our lives over time.

## MY JOURNAL: FEBRUARY 11, 2017

(New Beginnings women's event was established on January 21, 2012. It's a one-day event designed for women to relax, rejuvenate and renew their minds, bodies, and spirits.)

*It's here today!!!! Wow, 575 ladies are coming to my women's event! My ministry team pretty much took care of everything. I love them so much. They have such servant hearts. I know God is doing some amazing things in the lives of the ladies who come. Liz Curtis Higgs was amazing, I laughed so hard!*

*Jim decided to stay home. His son stayed with him Friday night and all-day Saturday.*

## MY JOURNAL: FEBRUARY 17, 2017

*Jim and I are needing some different scenery, so we are going to our favorite beach and eat at our favorite restaurants. So excited, but knowing life is no longer the same, and we will have to do things a bit differently.*

*We stopped every few hours to stretch our legs. Arrived at 4:00 pm. I noticed Jim was having trouble getting out of the car. He proceeded to hold his shoes and medicine in his hands. He dropped one of his shoes and lost his balance and hit his head on the hard pavement. I immediately called*

*911, because I saw this HUGE knot over his right eye. I took him to the hospital and decided to lance the knot, which took 10 stitches. So thankful it wasn't worse.*

## MY JOURNAL: FEBRUARY 18, 2017

*Jim's eye is completely closed today. He loves the sunbath so much when we are at the beach, so since we were on the first floor, we put a recliner chair for him to stretch out and get some sun. He was in hog heaven; except for the fact he could only see out of one eye. He's such a trooper. He never complains much about any situation. He bought this coffee mug that says "It is, what it is." I guess that sums it up!*

## MY JOURNAL: MARCH 8, 2017

*Appointment at Vanderbilt's ALS clinic today. Put Jim on some new meds to help him sleep. Jim shared with me today, he had quit taking his morning aspirin, hoping he would have a stroke, and he wouldn't have to go through the things this disease brings. My heart broke when I heard those words come from his mouth. The doctor suggested going to some counseling and said it's very normal for patients with terminal illnesses to think this way.*

The desire for a hastened death among terminally ill patients is not uncommon. Depression and hopelessness are the strongest predators in these situations. The best way to handle when these thoughts surface is to talk with a therapist or someone close to you. It is certainly understandable that sometimes the patient is thinking of being a burden to their caretaker.

Lord, please give us strength and courage to walk this journey. Please help him when his spirits are low and he feels helpless.

## My Journal: March 27, 2017

*Jim decided he wanted to look into the clinical trials at Emory in Atlanta. We are searching out every avenue for answers that might cure or slow down this dreaded disease.*

## My Journal: March 31, 2017

*Today 15 years ago, I was getting ready to marry this wonderful man God had given me. It's been an amazing ride, full of laughter, excitement, most of all, an abundance of love. Jim Jobe completes me. He makes me feel safe. He is the best part of me. So glad I said, "I Do."*

Beautiful memories are all we have when we lose a loved one. A part of our grief is being able to travel back to those good memories in order to move forward. Death does not stop us from loving those we lost. The love always stays with us. Every moment we have is the path we need to follow, to the light, the hope, and the dreams we have for our future.

## My Journal: April 8, 2017

*Camping was something we loved to do together. Sadly, today we sold it (the camper). Reality is that he can no longer handle it. He's having a really hard time accepting this. I wish I could fix this disease, but I know God is our only HOPE, and we trust HIM!*

## My Journal: April 9, 2017

*Today's worship service was great. Jim was able to go today. He sometimes says it hard to go, because it's so emotional for him. I had to have a "come to Jesus" meeting with Jim today about using his voice machine. I know it's not what he wants to do, but it's the best thing we have right now to communicate with each other. Please stay strong, Jim. Don't lose hope! I Love You!*

Faith is a powerful thing. It affects how we see the world, our communities, and our lives. Sometimes it's hard to have faith when our lives are shattered. God's Word says, "Faith is the substance of the things hoped for, the evidence of things not seen" Hebrews 11:1.

When we believe that God will fulfill His promises, we are showing true faith—even when we don't see evidence despite trusting in the character of God, believing His promises, and knowing His rewards are true. Faith keeps hope alive!

## My Journal: May 27, 2017

*Leaving for a family vacation with kids and grandchildren. I know it's not going to be the same this year with all the difficulties of walking and talking, but I wouldn't trade this time for anything. The car is packed to the ceiling with food and equipment, and the kids are flying in tomorrow.*

*Picture day tomorrow. Going to do a shot with all of us holding ice cream cones gathered around Jim. I can't wait for us all to be together as it may be our last beach trip together with "Granddaddy and Mimi" together.*

Much of our Joy happens on an emotional level. We all have emotions inside us all day long. Our feelings anchor our memories. It's so important to document those wonderful memories, whether by pictures, voice recordings, or movies. When someone you love becomes a memory, the memory becomes a TREASURE.

## My Journal: June 1, 2017

*Dreading the long drive home. Since Jim can no longer speak much, he tends to stay quiet, which makes the ride home even longer. I feel like he's retreating into himself. Not wanting to let me know how he's really feeling. Oh my gosh, I can't imagine what's going through his mind. He has been given a new voice machine, but he hates it. He has an app on his phone called text to speech which he uses a lot.*

## MY JOURNAL: JUNE 29, 2017

*Wow, what a day!!!!*
*I was just finally understanding I thought what's going on in Jim's mind.*
*We were so good at communicating our feelings, especially now. Then out*
*of the blue, we go to his doctor's office for a check-up and walk out with*
*Hospice papers. Jim said "I'm tired of going to the doctors, I want to live out*
*my last days on my own terms, going till I can't go anymore, surrounded by*
*those I love."*

I have read that many people with a terminal illness most likely want to die at home. That was a good read I saw in a magazine, but I never thought that would be my Jim's wishes. Jim was a bit of a stubborn man who was never good at budging on his convictions. So, I knew this was something he had thought long and hard about, and who was I to try to change his mind. Well, I believe at this point in someone's life, because we love them so much, we have to honor their wishes.

## MY JOURNAL: JULY 4, 2017

*Been a while since I have journalled. It's getting really hard to do anything*
*except take care of Jim. I have a new appreciation for caretakers. I'm ex-*
*hausted, mentally, physically, and spiritually. Even though it's terribly hard,*
*I'm so thankful I still have him with me.*

One of my biggest regrets is not taking care of myself through the process. Most women think no one can take care of their loved one as you can. That's probably somewhat a true statement, but I have witnessed some amazing nurses and home-health caretakers that have grown to love Jim in a special way.

Please take time to recognize the signs of emotional and physical fatigue. If the stress of caretaking is left unchecked, it can take a toll on your health, relationships, and state of mind. That's why taking care of yourself isn't a luxury; it's a necessity.

## My Journal: July 25, 2017

*Continuing to see Redbirds in my backyard. Not sure what God's trying to tell me, but I know He's here. Talking to his hospice nurse, Jennifer, about putting a B-pap on Jim at night. The oxygen in his nose is really not helping him. The muscle twitching in his arm is getting much worse.*

## My Journal: July 28, 2017

*Jim is not feeling well today. His nurse said she didn't know how he was still walking at all. He's made of sheer "Determination and Willpower," she said.*

## My Journal: July 29, 2017

*Jim continues to ride his recumbent bike. We bought this bike when his legs started giving out. But amazingly, he can still use it. It makes him happy and gives him a sense of freedom from this disease. He will ride it up and down the street, then into the church parking lot, then comes back home. I usually have to call a neighbor to help me peel his body off the bike. As much as he loves it, he is extremely exhausted and can't stand alone.*

## My Journal: July 30, 2017

*Jim's legs are not working well today. It's a wheelchair day instead of walker!*
*I took him to see his mom today. Neighbor had to help me get him into the car, probably going to be the last trip to Lewisburg. Afraid the wheels are coming off the bus. It makes me so sad. Lord, give me strength and give Jim peace.*

Facing moments like this was terribly hard. To know that life as I have always known was about to come to an end. There was nothing I could do or even change it. Jim has a coffee cup that says it all. "IT IS WHAT IT IS."

## My Journal: July 31, 2017

*I gave Jim his first morphine shot injection today. It really made him rest much better.*

## My Journal: August 6, 2017

*Planning to go see a movie with Jim's son:* Planet of the Apes! *Neighbors are bringing lunch today. So thankful for friends and church family who are helping with food. Last thing on my mind is to cook. Jim has seemed to get a second wind, and with his strong will and grit is able to walk some today.*

## My Journal: August 7, 2017

*A BIG BLUR!!!!! Bad Day.*

## My Journal: August 9, 2017

*Jim has slept a lot today. Canceled his massage and his pedicure. Jim had never had a pedicure before, but after Cindy had trimmed his toenails and rubbed his legs, he understands why we women love them so.*

## My Journal: September 10, 2017

*Things I'm afraid are changing for Jim. Lord help us in these days ahead. His legs have started spasming. He has been in terrible pain this morning. Alive Hospice came and spent 4 hours with us. I'm feeling so helpless. I have become such a fan of Alive Hospice. Their staff are living out their calling, with such love and affection for the patient and their family.*

Rather than seeking out a cure, hospice care provides to make someone's remaining time on earth as meaningful as possible. This may mean pain care or nursing care, but It also includes emotional support and help with everyday tasks. Hospice services can include respite care, where they offer the caregivers a short break to rest and recharge.

## MY JOURNAL: SEPTEMBER 11, 2017

*Jim had a terrible night. Tossing back and forth to get comfortable. His daughter and my son came today, and I was able to get some sleep.*

*His nurse told me I was probably looking at weeks for Jim. I can hardly breathe, when I think about my life without this man beside me. He is my soulmate, my best friend, the best of everything in this life. I know his future home is a place with no more pain and suffering, but my heart hurts just thinking about living mine without him.*

*Father, I ask in Jesus name that he doesn't suffer. Please let him pass from this life into your presence without much pain.*

## MY JOURNAL: SEPTEMBER 12, 2017

*Jim's mom and sister came today. Our pastor came and we had the Lord's Supper together. It was a sweet but emotional time.*

## MY JOURNAL: OCTOBER 9, 2017

*Finding it hard to write down my feelings right now. They are all over the place. Moved Jim's hospital bed into the family room this weekend. Another step to the final step! I know he knows this is the final spot for him. It kills me to see and hear him weeping, so all I can do is hold him!*

*I do understand why the move from our bedroom to the family room was emotionally draining. He is still of sound mind, so he understands this was just another move to the final destination, that being death. I'm trying really hard to not talk much about the process, just do it quickly and try to get his mind onto something else.*

*Father God, please give him peace and comfort as only you can.*

### MY JOURNAL: OCTOBER 14, 2017

*Jim's legs are getting very difficult to control with pain meds. Called Alive Hospice nurse and decided to take him to an in-patient facility. Wondering is this the last time he will be in our home?*

### MY JOURNAL: OCTOBER 15-18, 2017

*Jim's pain for the last few hours has been horrific. Doctor has upped pain meds. I never want him to experience that kind of pain again. Lord, please help him!*

### MY JOURNAL: OCTOBER 16-18, 2017

*These days we are strictly trying to manage his pain. Not getting much rest at all. Friends and family are coming by to show their love and support for us.*

### MY JOURNAL: OCTOBER 19, 2017

*I never realized how weary you can get without sleep, but I can't seem to leave him. Continue to keep Jim comfortable with meds.*

*Jim's mom is coming over today. I am going to speak with her about talking to Jim, telling him that it's OK to let go of this world. Later this afternoon she said she told him she would be OK and it was time to go to his new home in heaven.*

### MY JOURNAL: OCTOBER 20, 2017

*I had told the nurse I believed "Nanny" was the "key" to Jim leaving this earth. They told me they didn't see any signs of him passing any time soon. It may be a few more days. Just as I thought, they came in at 4:30 am and saw a huge change in Jim, and they thought death was getting closer. So, at*

*5:30, I called all the children and said to come on, that it wouldn't be much longer. They held his hand, and I laid my hand on his chest as he took his last breath at 6:15 am.*

It is an amazing feeling to actually fill someone's heartbeat stop, knowing that they just entered the presence of their Savior. I am extremely comforted knowing that when Jim took his last breath, he was in the presence of Almighty God. God promised us in His word, Romans 14:8, "If we live, we live for the Lord, and if we die for the Lord. So whether we live or die, we belong to the Lord." I knew he was experiencing a new home, a home that was built just for him. As Christ-followers, we live for that moment, to be with our Lord for eternity.

Isaiah 12:12 "I will trust, and NOT fear, for God is our strength."

# When You Feel Like Giving Up...

*G*od transforms the impossible into the possible.
He offers the unpromising a promise.
He gives strength to the weak.
He encourages the discouraged.
And yes--He specializes in miracles.

- Time-Warp Wife

## CHAPTER 3

# What About This Grief?

Most likely, we all have known grief to some degree. Even until the end, there was something inside me that said, "No, this really isn't happening." If Jim is gone, that will mean my future is one big without.

The loss of someone you love changes your entire life. It rocks your world, shakes your foundation and everything that was "right" immediately becomes unfamiliar.

Grief. What do you know about this emotion? Grief can be described as an "intense suffering and acute sorrow." In grief, the bottom falls out of your world.

Grieving is a process that sometimes is very disorderly. It is not on anybody's schedule, it won't fit your appointment book, and you have absolutely no control over it when it slaps you upside your head. It can deflate your peace and joy right out of you without any warning.

After Jim died, I found myself not even wanting to go to the store because I knew I would turn into a puddle of tears if anyone said a word to me. Later as I researched about grief, turning into a puddle at any moment was very natural.

Going through this experience led me to "The Three N's of Grief," and they have helped tremendously. Here they are:

- Grief is *normal* because it is how people respond to a loss. It's normal to expect people who've lost someone to be deeply affected by their loss.
- Grief is *natural* in that it's an entirely human thing to do. We can't avoid grief-it's built into us. We are created to love when we care for someone, and when we lose someone we love, we grieve.
- Grief is *necessary*. Grief provides a healthy way to cope with the loss and everything it means to us. Trying to ignore or avoid grief won't work.

The biggest lesson I can share with you is this: Give yourself permission to grieve. Next, you'll see that the feelings you're having are *normal*, *natural*, and *necessary*.

Matthew 5:4: "Blessed are those who mourn, for they shall be comforted."

"grief only exists
where love lived
first"
-Franchesca Cox

# CHAPTER 4

## When The Loss Sinks In

There is a point when the magnitude of your loss finally sinks in. The person you love really *did* die. He or she is not going to call today. The pain is so bad that our hearts just can't accept it.

Have you ever questioned your sanity during this time?

Those crazy feelings of intense grief sometimes are a sane reaction. A few examples that are all symptoms of normal grief:

- "Crazy" or irrational thoughts
- Fearful thoughts
- Feelings of despair or hopelessness
- Increased irritability
- Inability to concentrate
- Losing track of time
- Difficulty falling asleep and staying asleep
- Shattered beliefs about life, the world, and God

At times you may wonder if you're going to survive, or even if you want to. Any feeling is healthy because it means that you are truly feeling. You can only heal what you can feel. Many times, we stuff down our feelings, so those around us think we are handling it very well. The problem with this approach with grief is that grief cannot be healed if we are not honest about those feelings. Stuffing them can't heal them.

*I just can't remember a lot...*

*Just a typical Friday night, already had gone to bed, when I got that dreaded phone call that no parent wants to get. Then I heard my ex-wife on the other end saying, "Our daughter has had an accident."*

*One moment my little 16-year-old daughter was alive, and the next, she was GONE!*

*I remember being at the church, and I remember being at the graveside, but other than that, it's a fog. I believe I repressed it so much I didn't feel anything. I don't necessarily recommend repressing feelings, it's just the way I dealt with my loss. One thing I regret is that I didn't do some kind of counseling, that maybe could have brought my feelings more to light. Maybe then I could have experienced a bit more.*

*One thing I learned from this loss is "Never take anybody or anything for granted."*

Another approach to pain is to use your pain for good.

Sometimes the tragedy teaches us to value each day, appreciate the good moments, and get our priorities straight. We discover sometimes we have more power to do what we never thought we could do. Remember, even if we can't change the circumstances, we can change our attitudes.

> "Perhaps the most important truth I have learned is that healing in grief is heart-based, not head-based."
>
> —Alan Wolfelt

Grieving is like having broken ribs. On the outside you look fine, but with every breath, it hurts.

—

AUTHOR UNKNOWN

# Chapter 5

# The Gift of Tears

Death is like a thief in the night. It steals from us without warning. It takes our treasures that never can be replaced. It steals wedding dances, big hugs from our grandchildren, warm arms wrapped around a new baby. It steals away any future we might have had.

At times extreme joy can bring about tears. For me crying comes easy. I cry at weddings, funerals, movies, anything that has an emotional string tied to it. At times extreme joy can bring about tears. However, tears mostly result from excessive sorrow when too much pain is applied to our hearts. Yet, it's really amazing that when tears flow out, all the stressors within our bodies become light.

Karl Menninger of The Vital Balance says that "Weeping is perhaps the most human and universal of all relief measures."

After Jim died, it seemed like all I did was cry. My heart was broken into a million pieces.

Even though tears came easy for me, sometimes it's very difficult for others. When the tears begin to flow, you may feel uncomfortable, but tears are cleansing, and they release the tension of stress. They discharge whatever is in the heart.

James Miller, author of How Can I Help?, suggests the best way to handle your feelings is not to "handle" them but to feel them.

I highly suggest you find a safe place where no one can interrupt you and allow the tears to flow.

Ecclesiastes 3:4: "A Time to weep, and a time to laugh; a time to mourn, and a time to dance."

CHAPTER 6

# Is My Grief Normal?

Grief is the healing process that helps us deal with the loss of a loved one. Grief will ebb and flow throughout our life after a loss, and it is the result of loving. While we don't 'get over' the loss of someone, we do learn to live with that loss.

When we lose a loved one, almost everything in us and around us changes at the moment of their last breath. If you are like me and experienced intense grief and those "crazy" emotions, here are a few symptoms of normal grief I found to be helpful.

- Distorted thoughts
- Fearful thoughts
- Feelings of despair and hopelessness
- Want to talk a lot or not at all
- Memory lags or mental short circuits
- Losing track of time
- Increase or decrease of appetite and/or sexual desire
- Shattered beliefs about life, the world, and God
- Difficulty falling or staying asleep
- Inability to concentrate
- Obsessive focus on the loved one
- Numbed emotions

We'll take a look at these in the coming chapters. Just know that there's nothing wrong with grief, and there are ways to help you express it and work your way through it.

## COLLEEN'S STORY

*Friday, August 10th, was the worst day I have ever experienced. In an instant, everything around me changed. I had been at my new job a little over a week when I received a phone call from my husband to meet him at the hospital because our son had been in an accident. I happened to be out of town, so I was rushing to get there when I received a call from my boss insisting I stop by the office before going to the hospital.*

*I got into her car, and we proceeded to head out to the hospital. It was the quietest five-minute drive I've ever experienced. I was praying the whole time in the car. We arrived at the hospital's emergency room where I saw hundreds of friends lining the sidewalks. One of our friends, who was a police officer, escorted me to this tiny spot in the emergency room, where my husband was standing. He proceeded to tell me he had terrible news. Our son, Greg, was dead! I was in shock. I was confused. I didn't want to believe what he just said, that my 24-year-old son had committed suicide.*

*I couldn't wrap my brain around what has been said because Greg was living at home trying to buy his own home and make a better life for his six-year-old daughter Emma. He only wanted the best for her. He loved being around everybody. He loved to make people laugh and smile. He was an outstanding golfer. He was always willing to go that extra mile for anyone who needed help. So how could this happen?*

*He loved God and he went to church; how could Greg think this was his only way out?*

*Why didn't he reach out to one of his many friends? Why not me, his dad, his brother?*

*I admit it was embarrassing at times to admit my son had committed suicide. How could he not know that I was there for him!*

*All these things keep popping up in my head.*

*Greg always felt not quite good enough. In his golf, he thought he could have always done a bit better.*

*Many times I have looked back at pictures and wondered if he was truly happy in that picture or was he suffering in silence.*

*Looking back, I was surrounded by a large number of friends, but my faith is really what kept me standing. Both mine and my husband's faith was tested during this time.*

*Since my husband was the one who found our son's body hanging, it was extremely hard on him. He did CPR until the paramedics got there. I can't even imagine what his mind and heart was experiencing.*

*It was in that time my husband turned his back on God. How could a loving God allow something like this to happen?*

*I just had to cry out to God for me but also for my husband. I was scared I was losing him. I always have had this verse that from a small child was my go-to verse in times of distress. "I can do ALL things through Christ Jesus, who gives my strength." (Philippians 4:13)*

*I trusted God to help see me through this. No doubt in my mind that today I wouldn't be standing if I didn't believe God's promises to me.*

*I finally had to give it totally to God. He knew the bigger picture, and I didn't.*

I really became a recluse because I didn't want to run into anyone from church or work. I knew their first words would be, "How are you"? and I would instantly become a puddle on the floor. I knew they didn't know what to say, and everything was really awkward. It was also emotionally draining for me. I was heartbroken, and there was a hole in my heart that I knew was never coming back.

I'm lucky for the fact that my son had a daughter. She looks so much like him and says things that bring us joy every day.

Grief is such a part of this journey that I experience in some way every day.

The grief I experienced the first month was as followed:

- Wasn't myself
- Almost out of body experience—when people would come over, it was almost like I was above looking down on them
- Couldn't stand to be alone
- Felt anger
- Blamed myself-why didn't I know God was in control then and is in control now
- Blamed others
- Constant turmoil

It has now been eight years and my grief has changed a bit.

- I still grieve a little bit every day
- I'm a bit more at peace with everything
- I knew he was in control then, and I know he's in control now
- I can now talk about it more
- I don't get as upset when I hear his name
- I can now smile when we talk about memories

*I was asked what has been my biggest surprise in the healing process of grief?*

*I tried to lay blame on others, only to realize I could never get past anything until I learned to forgive others that might have played a part in this. It's only by God's grace and mercy I've been able to let those feelings go.*

*I always had the common fears that come along with the "firsts." First Christmas, first birthdays, etc.*

*We had a friend who reached out to my husband, who had lost a child and made a wonderful suggestion that we did the first Christmas. We contacted all our son's buddies and asked them to write down a precious memory about our son and put it in his stocking and read it Christmas day. It was such a comfort to recognize just how many lives he did touch.*

*One thing I would like to say to those out there who are wondering what to say to those of us who are grieving, as I do recognize it's an awkward time: Please, please, please never be afraid to say their name!*

*It won't make us sad by reminding us they died; believe me we know. We just don't ever want them to be forgotten.*

*As time heals, hearing their names brings comfort to our hearts!*

*For those dealing with or know someone dealing with suicide two things I want you to know, (1) suicide is permanent and (2) Help is available.*

*Suicide is the 10th leading cause in the U.S. In 2018 48,344 Americans died by suicide. On the average, there are 132 suicides per day.*

*National Suicide Prevention Line: 1-800-273-8255*

If you find yourself struggling, here are a few scriptures I found helpful:

> Psalm 4:8 "I will lie down and sleep in peace, for you alone, O Lord, make me dwell in safety."

> Psalm 94:19 "Lord, when doubts fill my mind, when my heart is in turmoil, quiet me and give me renewed hope and joy."

> Hebrews 13:5-6 "Never will I leave you; never will I forsake you. The Lord is my helper; I will not be afraid."

> Note to Self: I'm NOT broken, I am normal.

> Proverbs 3:24 "When you lie down, you will not be afraid: when you lie down your sleep will be sweet"

CHAPTER 7

# Working Through The First Years

It's funny how you never think of having a meltdown, much like your two-year-old grandson, but many friends informed me about the dreaded "year of the firsts."

I can vividly recall the many firsts after my husband passed and how someone could just look at me and I would become a puddle of tears. The first birthday, first Father's Day, first Christmas, the first time I went to church alone, and so on. Each first ended with me thinking, "He's not here."

The entire year was filled with constant reminders that my soulmate was never coming back. Nothing in my life flowed the same. Nothing felt the same. Nothing would ever be the same.

I've listed a few things that I really didn't expect on this fresh journey through grief that I wish someone had told me about, in the hopes that it might help you.

- Grief attacks: these are intense surges of grief that happens when you least expect it. They are disruptive and can leave you standing in a puddle of tears, just by someone saying, "how are you today?"
- Expect feelings of exhaustion: After a loss, many times people return to work, school, or other activities feeling less confident, less able to concentrate, and flooded by memories that will disrupt your thinking. For some people, work becomes a place to take their minds off the loss for a while.
- It's very common to have difficulty sleeping, a change in appetite, and possible weight loss. Be sure to speak to your doctor about these symptoms, and know it is perfectly ok to take medicine to help you get through this time.
- Expect "if only" and "should haves." Many times, a person may not have had a chance to say good-bye or resolve unfinished business between them. You may regret doing or not doing something. It helps to talk to someone you trust about your concerns. There are many groups that can walk this journey with you, or you might be drawn to someone who has experienced a loss much like yours. And remember, no one can totally understand your grief, your questions, or what your loss has meant to you. Each person's grief is unique and their own.

## JODI'S STORY

*I stayed up really late last night, maybe subconsciously, to avoid waking up to today. One year ago, today, I lost my husband. I hate that sentence. I hate the part before the comma and I certainly hate the part after the comma. I hate today. I hate the memories of a year ago today.*

*As I slept, I reached for his hand, and it wasn't there to hold. That startled me awake.*

*The above perfectly summarizes the beginning of year two, too. The start of the second year has also caused me to pause and reflect back on my first year as a widow. I needed to identify any progress I made in order to figure out how I am going to deal with my sophomore year in grief. So here it is boiled down to ten things I learned in my first year as a widow.*

### 1. Survival is possible.

*The first days and weeks after losing my husband, I wasn't sure how I'd survive, or if I even wanted to. Losing my spouse crumbled my foundation and the pain was unbearable at times. I look back now and see that although it wasn't pretty, it serves as proof that I can do hard things. I came, I saw, and I got through it? This is mostly because I HAD to, not because of some phenomenal strength of character. But nevertheless, I survived.*

### 2. My "Inner Circle" has changed.

*I really struggled with disappointment and hurt over the loss of what I thought I somehow deserved from friends. When they fell short, I felt abandoned. I'm looking back today with a little more "extra grace." Instead of clinging to hurt, I recognize with gratitude the new people that have emerged in my life. The people who are genuinely concerned about me, the people who are sincerely praying for me and selflessly wrapping me in their love, support, and friendship, have risen to the top like rich cream.*

*So instead of dwelling in the hurt of relationships lost, I'm focusing on the new, beautiful people God has put on my path. I'm getting better at letting go of hurt, disappointment, and negativity. I'm trying to be less selfish about the shake-up of my inner circle.*

## 3. The pain doesn't lessen.

Although it's true that maybe I cry softer and maybe even less frequently, the pain hasn't really lessened. In many ways, it's intensified. It's not gone, just changed. There's been a little bit of getting used to pain in this first year, although my heart is far from calloused. My wound still bleeds, but there aren't as many new "cuts."

## 4. I will not ever be the same person again.

At the one-year mark, I've realized the old me is gone. She died with my husband. In her place, there is emerging a new, changed person that begs to be discovered. She's slightly familiar but not quite the fully recognizable me from the past. Year two is going to be about finding her and giving her what she needs.

## 5. You will miss them more now.

In many ways, I miss my husband more today than I did early on. Looking in the face of year two, I see more reality than year one revealed. I see a long road ahead without him. This new truth is a very lonely one. I guess year one knew I couldn't handle all of the revelations at once, so it saved plenty for year two.

## 6. Memories fade.

I knew this would happen, but it's still so difficult. I write about my husband, talk to my kids about their Dad, and yet lately, it's harder to remember certain things about him. When one of the kids asks to hear a story, my mind finds fewer stories to share. I'm sure memories will resurface at different times in life, but I want to have access to every single one at any given time. When I can't recall something like the smell on his shirt, the sound of his voice, or his laugh, it hurts. I don't want to lose those memories, and yet, they fade.

## 7. Other people's grief, loss, and pain affect me greater than before.

*Losing my husband has given me new lenses. I am now keener to the pain of other grievers. When I hear of someone who has lost their child, their spouse, their parent, etc., my heart isn't just heavy, it's shattered for them. My pre-widow self wasn't able to sympathize in the same ways. The brand-new grievers with raw, fresh pain stay on my heart and in my prayers for months and months. Before, I would've paused, maybe attended a funeral and sent a card and then life would've swept me forward. Now, I think of them daily.*

## 8. Depression is a real thing, and faith is still a choice.

*Other widows have warned me about year two. They've told me it's worse than year one. I don't know yet if that will be true for me, but I can tell you that my depression really set in the closer I got to year two. It's real and it's a suppressive joy-stealing demon. I don't like that I need help with this, but I do. I refuse to be stifled by its grip on me, so I'll fight it every way I know how. Depression isn't about not having enough faith. It isn't about choosing joy over sadness. It isn't about digging deeper. It isn't mind over matter. It's a real thing, no matter how much faith you have. There's no shame in getting help for it.*

*And speaking of faith, it has been tested this year. I haven't lost it, but there have been many times where I've disengaged from God because, sometimes, I can't feel Him with me anymore. Sometimes I can't feel His comfort, and I'm left with a decision to trust His promises and follow Him anyway. I've chosen to do that, but I want to admit it hasn't been easy. At times I've been very lonely, angry, and desperate for His answers. I've longed for a glimpse of His plan for me now, and I don't have it yet. I continue to seek Him, but I wanted to confess this year has been a faith-tester, for sure.*

## 9. There are still moments that come out of nowhere and take my breath away.

*Time doesn't heal all wounds, and it doesn't make the heart and mind any smarter. There's evidence of this almost every day. Maybe it's something the kids say or do that makes me happy or proud, or maybe it's something I'm afraid of and need help working through, and for a millisecond, I think about calling or texting my husband to share the moment with him or to seek his help. These swift moments are the mind trickery that continues to steal my breath away. It's cruel how at my core I still can't always remember that he's gone. I'm living proof that grief amnesia is a real thing.*

## 10. There's no more time for BS.

*When loss cracks you wide open and leaves you raw and exposed, you quickly learn what's worth hard work and emotional energy and what's not. Year one has revealed there's no room for BS and drama in my life anymore. It has taught me the importance of focusing on things that really, truly matter. I really know now how fleeting our time on earth is, and I am determined to make it count.*

*I still don't know what the future holds for me, but I am determined to make my life matter. I want to love more, laugh more, help more, stand up for the weak more, hold the hands of the hurting more and appreciate the small moments more. It's still a long road ahead, one I can't look down for very long periods of time. Heading into year two, it's still a very one-day at a time scenario. It will be at my own pace. Sometimes that pace will be slow and painful, and sometimes, I'll surge ahead with speed. But I'll keep moving forward, one step at a time.*

*Jodi's Blog, Extragracerequired.com, is a great resource that I recommend you check out.*

As I worked my way through the first year, I struggled with all that might come. Looking back on that time, I want you to know that it's possible to hurt, feel pain, and make small amounts of progress at the same time.

## MY JOURNAL: NOVEMBER 4, 2017

*Headed to Seagrove Beach to stay with friends for a week. Wish I could say I'm looking forward to it, but it's the beginning of many first "withouts" Jim. It's my first time to fly alone. But as always God goes before me to prepare the way. I had the nicest stewardess, who took extra good care of me. I never wanted to be in this club, but I'm here, so I have to walk gracefully for those who will follow in my paths.*

## MY JOURNAL: NOVEMBER 7, 2017

*Didn't sleep well last night. Reading some books I got on grief. Finding out grief hits when you least expect it.*

## MY JOURNAL: NOVEMBER 10, 2017

*Heading back from beach. I had wonderful weather, good food, lots of laughter with friends, but one thing was missing—my precious Jim.*

*I found myself everyday wanting to talk with him about something or wanting him to just sit and watch the sunset with me. It wasn't the same, just as it will be when I get home. He's not there and he's never coming back. I know he would be saying, "Cherie, you must go on living, one day you will come and be in this beautiful place too."*

*Today is Jim's birthday. So many mixed emotions. Visited his grave and brought balloons. Family signed messages on them and released them into heaven. Know it's a celebration going on in heaven, but it's still pretty sad for those of us left behind.*

*Jim's favorite was a Sonic chocolate milkshake, so we all went and had one in Jim's honor .I believe Jim is smiling down on all who were there today. He loved his family so, and always wanted everyone to be happy.*

There is a lot of information out there on grief. Some of it I found to be helpful, some of it to be more myths than reality. Please take comfort in knowing that you don't have to grieve just the way "experts" say you should. You are your own person and it's ok to be that way.

Let's take a look at some of those myths now.

When a train goes through a tunnel and it gets dark, you don't throw away the ticket and jump off. You sit still and trust the engineer. Trust God today no matter how dark your situation. God says, "You are coming out."

CHAPTER 8

# Myths of Grief

**Myth #1: Grief follows a logical, linear pattern**

There is no right or wrong way or time frame for grieving. Each person's grief is uniquely his or her own and it is neither predictable nor orderly. While stages of grief have been identified, it is not helpful to try to tell somewhat what their grief and mourning experiences should be or to try to fit our own grief into a nice, neat package.

Grief is the internal thoughts and feelings we feel when we experience a loss. Mourning, on the other hand, is taking the internal feelings of grief and expressing it outside ourselves.

**Myth #2: Moving on with life means you forget about the loved one who died**

Moving on means you've accepted the reality of your loved one's death. That is not the same as forgetting. Finding ways to honor him or her while creating a new life allows you to keep your loved one's memory as a part of you. As new opportunities emerge, you are able to make commitments to the future, realizing that the person who died will never be forgotten, and knowing that your life can and will move forward.

## Myth #3: The goal is to 'get over' grief

We live in a society that is both afraid of death and afraid of emotions. We are not encouraged to express our emotions, and many people view grief as something to get over rather than experience. The result is that many people either grieve in isolation or attempt to run away from their grief.

The problem with trying to mask or move away from grief is that it results in internal anxiety and confusion. Grief is a process, and moving that along too fast or denying the normal pain can cause people to think their thoughts and feelings are abnormal. The goal is to go through the experience and move forward into a new reality.

## Myth #4: It is important to have a strong outer appearance

Trying to ignore your pain or keep it from surfacing can only make it worse. The energy it takes to try and do this will result in far greater pain. For healing to occur, it is necessary to face your grief and actively deal with it.

It is really the pain of the loss that we want to avoid. Because of that, allowing those natural feelings of sadness, loneliness, anger, etc. to move through you is one key to that healing. You don't need to "protect" your family or friends by putting on a brave front. Showing your true feelings can help them and you.

## Myth #5: Friends and family should not bring up the subject of grief and loss

People who are grieving usually want and need to talk about their loss. Having close family and friends initiate the conversation can make it easier for people to talk about. In reality, many people in our culture grieve, but they do not mourn. Instead of being encouraged to express their grief outwardly, they are often greeted with messages such as "carry on," "keep your chin up," and "keep busy." So, they end up grieving within themselves in isolation, instead of mourning outside of themselves in the presence and support of loving companions.

Tim's story below shows the reality of grieving while understanding how to continue living (but not forgetting) when we lose a loved one.

## TIM'S STORY

*The first time I knew something was going on with my wife was New Year's 2017. She started itching; hands itching, feet itching. She went to the doctor and they noticed her eyes were very yellow also. They proceeded to do an MRI and cat scan and found she had a tumor in her bile duct, which is part of the liver. She didn't seem very worried at the time, but I knew this news just could not be good. We proceeded to get an appointment with a doctor at Vanderbilt, and by that time it was already stage four. That was on February 13th.*

*As my wife received this diagnosis, she told the doctor, "I'm gonna beat this," and his response was, "I've never seen anybody survive this type of cancer." And immediately, her response was, "Well, you don't know my God."*

*Immediately we started chemo in March until maybe July. The test showed the chemo was helping her jaundice, and she actually was feeling better.*

*We decided that since things were looking up, we would go on a cruise. She had a great time!*

*She wasn't a crier, but on the cruise, she let her emotions out. She was always thinking of others, and she knew this was hurting all the people she cared about. She was selfless!*

*We tried not to think about how cancer was attacking her body by living every day to the fullest. She wanted life to be as normal as possible.*

*Totally out of the blue one day she started having seizures. Soon we would discover she had brain tumors that had developed. She lived only six weeks after that.*

*I'm so thankful I had a good support team around me, that consisted of family and friends.*

*After the funeral, my heart was broken into a million pieces, wondering if I would ever be joyful again. As I began my new journey, there were days I wondered if I would ever breathe again.*

*As time progressed a bit and I began to embrace my new normal, I started doing things I always loved. Unfortunately, I had this sense of heavy guilt about going on with my life without her here.*

## MY JOURNAL: DECEMBER 1, 2017

*We are heading into the season of Joy and Hope, but somehow, I don't feel either.*

*Went to the doctor today to get an injection in my back. I was approached with my 1st "without." I could no longer check "married," I had to check "widow."*

Grieving requires an enormous amount of energy but pretending that you're not grieving requires even more.

You may begin to sense that your world is anxious for you to get on with your life. No one seems to understand that this is your new normal, and you're trying hard to get on with it. Many times, you'd like to say, "This is it, folks, like it or not."

Then other times you put your mask on and perform like a trained seal, just to keep what's normal in your life from leaving you.

Sue Catherine Holtkamp, PH. D, has a book you might find helpful: *Grieving with Hope: A personal Journey*

Joshua 1:9 "Do not be discouraged for the Lord your God will be with you wherever you go"

# Grief

never ends...
But it changes.
It's a passage,
not a place to stay.
Grief is not a sign
of weakness, nor
a lack of faith...
It is the price of love.

CHAPTER 9

# Coping With Loneliness

The loneliness of grief is one of the most gut-wrenching feelings I have ever experienced. I believe the worst part is coming home every day to an empty house. For months I would stay out till all the stores would close, just so all I had to do was to go to bed when I got home.

Constant reminders of your loved one linger all around. The empty bed, an empty place at the table, no one to share exciting news with, that phone call that says "I love you."

Naturally, loneliness is part of the grief scenery. Now that our loved one is gone, we must take charge of our feelings. We must not sink into self-pity or feelings of helplessness. We must commit to finding positive, healthy ways to fight these feelings of loneliness.

Here are a few ideas for connecting with other people when you're ready:

- Visit a support group (either a group or one on one)
- Start exercising or walking with a friend
- Call someone who you know that has experienced a loss
- Reintroduce yourself to groups and hobbies that you have an interest in
- Become a mentor or help with your favorite charity

- Volunteer at a homeless shelter, hospital, or soup kitchen
- Give yourself permission to be happy again

These positive acts of kindness will have a lasting impact on the lives of others while helping you meet new people.

Grieving is a grueling process, so there is no need to rush through it. Just try to be as loving, patient, forgiving and gentle with yourself as possible.

## MIKE'S STORY

*My wife, Lisa, was an incredible woman of faith. We called our journey "A Journey of Hope."*

*Lisa and I met my junior year in college. Obstacles presented themselves early, since Lisa was in high school. I consider myself lucky that Lisa would even look my way. She finally came to her senses, and we married on March 18, 1982. Life wasn't always perfect, but we managed to raise two amazing boys.*

*We also got our heartstrings pulled on with two amazing grandchildren.*

*It was October 2015 when this disease reared its ugly head. Her first sign that something was wrong was a raspy sound in her voice.*

*Lisa was always very active. She ran in four marathons that year. Despite the raspy sound, her body was still physically able to do pretty much anything she wanted. We began to seek out doctors and specialists to find out what the heck was going on. A preliminary diagnosis from one of the doctors said it could possibly be ALS. All I knew it was a disease that people started getting paralyzed. I was certain it wasn't ALS because it had nothing to do with losing your voice.*

ALS is a disease where the cells that control the muscles die, then the muscles die, and then the person becomes paralyzed. The only person I had ever heard of having this was the famous baseball player Lou Gehrig.

The following summer of 2016, we went on several vacations. Lisa's voice continued to decline, but her body remained intact. Also, in September 2016, we went to Vanderbilt Clinic's neurological unit where Lisa underwent many tests looking for possible signs of ALS. Lisa passed those tests with flying colors, so my thoughts were, "Thank God, she doesn't have ALS."

The doctor had one last test to perform, and it was on her reflexes. Unfortunately, he said her reflexes were too excited, which meant she did indeed have ALS. My heart sank as I couldn't believe this incredible woman had this wicked disease.

Lisa was the type of woman who wasn't going to let this possibility of this disease get her down. She continued to be active. After the diagnosis, we NEVER had another normal moment.

We knew this journey was scary, with lots of uncertainties, but we knew we were going through it together.

The doctors at Vanderbilt Clinic really didn't give us any hope. There just weren't any medications, trials, or anything else that could help this wicked disease. I now understand why they don't want to give you any false hope because nobody ever gets better with this disease. My personality is not one to sit around and do nothing, so I immediately got on the internet and found a place in Bangkok, Thailand, that was doing stem cell research. The cost was $40,000. A Go-Fund-Me account was set up. Hundreds of friends, family, and people we didn't even know raised funds in about 10 days.

*The hospital in Thailand was first class. They had a wing dedicated to stem cell research. We thought this was going to be the answer!*

*When we returned home, Lisa continued the regimen of medicines and special therapies to try to arrest the disease. She continued to keep her great sense of humor and was blessed that her body was still in great shape. Shortly she began to choke a lot and eventually wasn't able to eat. We had to make the decision to put a feeding tube in her stomach. I truly felt we were in the eye of a storm.*

*Ryan Stevens wrote a beautiful song called "In the Eye of the Storm." The chorus says, "You alone are the anchor when my sails are torn...Your love surrounds me, in the eye of the storm."*

*Lisa's prayer was always to encourage others, no matter what the situation, that with Christ, you can always experience HOPE, Courage, Peace and Strength to face this world's challenges.*

*Lisa's motto was "It's Not About Me, It's Not About this Disease, It's All About Leading Others to Christ." Through all of this, Lisa never complained or questioned God or asked, "Why me?"*

*Lisa left her earthly home and entered her heavenly home at 4:00 pm July 12th, 2018.*

We are reminded at times that our lives are much bigger than what we can see in front of us. Many times, lives are eternally changed because of the death of our loved ones. As Christ-followers, we are on display for all the world to see. People watch how we handle death. We will forever miss our loved one on this earth, but for a Christ-follower, it is a glorious time and a transition time to our eternal home.

CHAPTER 10

# Take Care of Yourself

No one really understands nor anticipates the physical, emotional, and spiritual toll grief takes unless you have experienced it yourself.

Grief taxes the immune system, making it easier to get ill. Physical symptoms can include headaches, fatigue, appetite loss, heart palpitations, and insomnia. The overall feeling is exhaustion.

Now is the perfect time to remember all those fitness guidelines, like eating balanced meals, taking vitamins, resting, and exercising on a regular schedule.

I get it that at the beginning of this grief process, you have little to no desire to take care of yourself. Some days it's hard to even get out of bed!

Sometimes you just need time alone to process what you're feeling and to remember the memories, and dream about what the future might look like.

During this time of grieving, you can't expect to feel "normal."

It will never be normal again. It will just be different. Know that one day you will survive and recover, having learned many valuable lessons you too can share with someone else.

After all, taking care of yourself is what our loved one would want us to do, and it's what we can do to continue on as best as we can.

So, get up-dress up-show up! One day you will embrace all this life has to offer!

"God promises to make something good out of the storms that bring devastation to your life."

—Romans 8:28

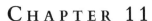

CHAPTER 11

# Rebuilding My Life (Will I Choose to Be a Caterpillar or a Butterfly?)

Please keep in mind, rebuilding the "New You" is not a dirty word!

It does NOT mean you've abandoned or forgotten your loved one. You are NOT being forced to choose between living again and remembering your loved one. They will always claim a place in your heart.

Rebuilding stretches you and makes you more awake to life and makes you more awake to life and the beautiful surroundings right in front of you. Some may be slow to happen, and some will happen overnight. But, all of them will help you gain great clarity on the "new you."

Unfortunately, you, along with many others, didn't sign up to walk this journey. The rebuilding of your future will be determined by how well you embrace what's in front of you. Perspective, patience, and determination are keys to your success!

Richard Bach wrote:" What the caterpillar calls the end of the world, the master calls a butterfly."

I wonder, how will you choose to rebuild your life? Will you remain a caterpillar or become a beautiful butterfly?

The morning began like so many other mornings. My husband had left the house for his daily six-mile run while I lingered over my second cup of coffee. I have always claimed the early hours for my personal time. My first cup of coffee had only one job to wake me up to the new day. It was always the second cup that helped me plan all activities.

Holding the cup with both hands, I would stroll throughout the house, making mental notes of my everyday chores. I stopped in the kitchen and placed my favorite coffee cup in the sink. I knew my husband would be home soon, so I began making breakfast. It would be more like brunch because my husband's yearly physical checkup was scheduled for that morning. Undoubtingly, he would be starved since he had nothing to eat or drink after our evening meal.

WE both regarded these physical examinations as a waste of time. My husband was the healthiest person you could ever meet. He was never sick. He exercised regularly, ate cleanly, never smoked, always drank in moderation, and took health seriously. My contribution would be to make him the biggest egg white vegetable omelet the world had ever seen.

As I was slaving away in the kitchen, I heard the garage doors open and my husband's car pulled into his usual spot. I continued with my surprise brunch but never heard the car door open. I imagined he was talking either business or deer hunting with one of his buddies. As he entered the kitchen, I turned around to congratulate him on yet another perfect health score.

As I turned, with an omelet in hand, I saw him staring at me. His expression was unusual: a half-smile and a half-paralyzed gaze. I immediately questioned him on the results of the checkup. He replied, "They said I have 12 months to live." I could not move. My eyes searched his glaring face for any clues as to what he was saying. My mouth opened to speak, *but no sounds could escape. Then, I heard a desperate plea slip through my lips. "What did you just say?"*

*Suddenly, the corners of his mouth turned up, and we both started laughing. My husband replied, "It's nothing, sweetheart. The Doc wants me to retake a few tests tomorrow. Something weird was obviously going on with the test equipment." We both sat down at the kitchen table and had a wonderful brunch together.*

*The next day came with great expectations. My husband left the house for the second round of tests. This time we would get the actual true results, the doctor assured.*

*My husband returned after several hours at the doctor's office. I heard his car pull into the garage like a thousand times before, but something felt different. I waited in the hallway facing the garage door. He opened the back door and slowly walked into the house. His head was bent down. His eyes faced the floor. Then ever so calmly, he raised his head and looked at me. He didn't say a word. He didn't have to. I ran into his arms and we both started crying together.*

*Cancer is the beast. We went to every Cancer client or institution in the United States. At the end of a very difficult journey, my husband went home to be with the Lord. He had found Christ in the midst of suffering and shared his faith with many in our community. I said goodbye to him, knowing he was in paradise. How wonderful for him. No more pain or suffering. No more worries or stress. No more money problems, health issues, mortgages, food costs, insurance price increases, automobile issues, credit card debt, or loneliness. How wonderful for him!*

*But what about me? Where was I going to live? How was I going to manage? I hadn't worked outside the home in a long time. Would anyone hire me? I am sixty years old. Will I ever feel like myself again? Will I ever be happy again? Do sixty-year-old women even date? Oh, my goodness, I hated dating when I was young. I cannot imagine how awful dating will be at this stage of life. Somebody just shoot me!*

*The first year goes by so quickly you hardly notice how lonely you really feel. There is much to do after a loved one dies. If you have lost a spouse, then you understand. After all the necessary legal systems had been satisfied, I stayed busy doing nothing. I found a hundred charities or women's groups to join. Nonprofit organizations are more than happy to put you to work helping others. That's all good and needed, but my question is, "who is helping you?" For me, I stayed over-committed on purpose. If I had zero personal time, then I had zero time to think about myself and my pain.*

*Up until this season of my life, every waking minute was directed to the care of my very sick husband. My days and several nights were completely occupied with a single purpose. To keep my husband alive. To keep my husband comfortable. To keep my husband fed, bathed, groomed, encouraged, and of course, entertained. This has become our new way of living, and I am forever grateful for this time. We shared every minute together. All 24 months, all 730 days, all 17,520 hours. Then he died. Now, I have no routine. More than that, I had no purpose. I lost more than a husband. I lost myself.*

*The second year comes, and still I have not cried. I have a new home, and I bought a sports car. Don't judge me. It was a cute little white Lexus convertible. I know, but it made complete sense at the time. I also made new friends. Not all of your couple friends will include you in the same events or parties you enjoyed before you were a widow. They still love you. They just do not know what to do with you as a single woman. Keep your friendships focused on the women and don't worry about the coupled parties.*

*I moved back to the town where most of my family still lived. My recently purchased 3-bedroom 2-and-a-half bath ranch style home was in need* of a complete overhaul. My new favorite word: projects. Painting, wallpapering, staining, new furniture, new draperies, landscaping were only a few of my "New Busy."

Meanwhile, my new friends were hard at work finding Mr. Right, but I had little interest. Not because I liked being alone but because I didn't feel single. Reluctantly, I agreed to go out on a blind date. Interesting phrase "Blind Date." I often wonder who is blind: the date or the friend fixing you up.

Dating at its best is horrible. So, after several uneventful blind dates, I decided to take matters into my own hands and do the unthinkable: I joined a dating website. Actually, my college-age granddaughters talked me into the enlistment. They assured me it was the modern way to meet my perfect match. I should probably tell you that I have little computer skills. Why I thought I would enjoy a computer dating site is beyond my comprehension. I do, however, know many women who enjoy this style of dating. Clearly, they have more skills than this ol' girl.

I did have several "hits" on my site, and being the gracious Southern lady, I felt obligated to respond to each visitor. I cannot begin to count how many polite refusals I typed in one night, all night. Too much for me. I later was told you do not have to respond if you are uninterested. I wish I had known that before the midnight hour. My eyes were bloodshot, and my fingers numb.

I did meet a man online who seemed charming and very handsome. We met for dinner in my town. When I walked in, I could not find him. His picture was in my mind and I quietly searched the small room in the front of the restaurant. Suddenly, from the back of the room, a man I did not recognize jumps up and shouts my name.

It was my date but looked nothing like his picture. Not even close. He was very polite and eager to be seated. We ordered dinner and began to *talk about ourselves. I should correct that statement. He talked about himself all night. I have never been so happy to skip dessert in my entire life. Before we parted ways, I asked him when he took the picture for the site. He explained that his site photo had been taken over 20 years ago. I asked him why not a recent photo, and he said, "Well, that one looks so much better." Am I the only one who sees something wrong here?*

*The third year gets better: My house remodeling is complete, and friends and family are settled firmly in my life. I have started working some and brought my charity work into a more normal time frame. I love my church family and even started a bible study in my house. I think less about my aloneness and more about the incredible blessings that surround my life. I spend time alone with the Lord and never hesitate to bring all my concerns to my Heavenly Father. I look at photos of my past life with my husband and cry like a baby. They are not tears of pain from my loss, but rather sweet reminders that I had something very few will ever know.*

*I am no longer angry or fearful. My thoughts are no longer centered around what I lost; rather, they are centered around what I have found. Faith has brought me into such a wonderful and fulfilling place. I love nothing more than to help other women find the peace and joy that only Christ gives. I know that my life is full, and should Jesus decide to add someone to it, I will be ready.*

*The fourth year and I am still alone, but I am not lonely. I have come to peace with my life, and my life is completely at peace with me. I decided to try dating again. A sweet friend of mine called to invite me to a cookout. She explained that she met a wonderful age-appropriate man and wants me to meet him. My friend sees herself as a Matchmaker, so to speak. Of course, I laughed at her and said, "not a chance, I am fine, really." My friend insists I give it a shot. The worst thing that could happen is I just met a really nice person.*

*This wonderful age-appropriate man has no idea he's being set up. The night of the cookout arrives and I could not be more nervous. I do what any normal nervous female would do and I skip the party! The next day the wonderful age-appropriate man calls me to introduce himself. I think it was the sound of his voice that first drew me to him. His voice was calming to my spirit. He was funny and we talked for a while. Then he invited me out for dinner. The next day I felt completely confident about our date.*

*I wasn't concerned about him being "Mr. Right," I was simply delighted to meet the man behind such an incredible voice. Our date was what all romantic movies should look like. I felt as if we had been friends our whole lives. He had lost his wife two years prior. It was never difficult discussing our past lives. We both had lost a great deal. Yet, there was an air of hope in the conversation. We made it through life, death, and dinner. That was September 2019. It is now November 2020. I am happy to announce today is our sixty-week Anniversary!*

*Never in a million years did I ever expect to love again. I was completely in love with my Savior. I had stopped searching for a person to make me feel whole. I am made whole through the Lord Jesus Christ.*

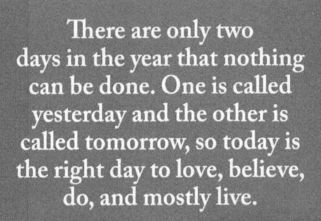

There are only two
days in the year that nothing
can be done. One is called
yesterday and the other is
called tomorrow, so today is
the right day to love, believe,
do, and mostly live.

–Dalai Lama

## CHAPTER 12

# You Are Not Alone in The Storm

Life is full of storms. You've been in them, and so have I.

A few years back, Jim and I were on one of our camping trips. It happened to be a beautiful day. Jim was catching fish right and left. Suddenly, he came running to me yelling," We gotta get back to camp!"

Just a few minutes later, we were fighting 30 mile-an-hour winds. He had anchored down the awning but was not quite sure if it was going to hold. Then all of a sudden, we heard this crash sound and looked out the window only to see our next-door neighbor's awning flying completely off their camper.

We asked ourselves, "Where did the storm come from?" One moment the skies were clear; the next, we were in a torrential rainstorm.

Storms are like that. They always appear out of nowhere, and always at the most inconvenient times, like outdoor weddings, outdoor graduations, outdoor ball games, they always disrupt our plans.

We are fortunate to have weather forecasters that can help us sometimes prepare for what's coming, but even then, some storms come without any warning at all.

Storms can rattle our beliefs as much as the wind can rattle our windows. Storms also have this way of shaking us to the core of what we believe. I don't know about you, but I don't want to be alone in a storm.

It's during this time, this storm of grief, that I have to draw my strength from my faith. It's the only reassuring and comforting thing that I have to hold on to. When God allows us to go through these storms, it's His hope that we will grow in our faith. Just know that some days bring sunshine, and some days bring storms.

Hold on to these verses and remind yourself that "He will never leave you."

Isaiah 41:10 "Fear not, for I am with you: be not dismayed, for I am your God: I will strengthen you, I will help you, I will uphold you with my righteous right hand."

Matthew 28:20 "Teaching them to observe all that I have commanded you. And behold, I am with you always, to the end of the age."

Joshua 1:9 "Have I not commanded you? Be strong and courageous. Do not be frightened, and do not be dismayed, for the Lord your God is with you wherever you go."

## BECKY'S STORY

*My pregnancy with Korley was not any different from my first child. Korley was born on February 4, 1999, and weighed 8 pounds.*

*One day I noticed Korley had a bit of cradle cap, so I decided to give her a bath to help get rid of it. I proceeded to take a small brush to try to remove the cradle cap. The next morning, I picked her up from her bassinet and noticed these huge blood blisters on top of her scalp. They were the size of a nickel in diameter.*

*Having worked in a lab, I knew that wasn't normal. I had learned a lot about blood cancer. The blisters did not go away, so I made an appointment with our pediatrician. He said it didn't look normal, so I immediately saw his wheels in his mind turning. He had an abdominal ultrasound and a complete blood count done. Her white blood cells were out the roof! Normal is 3,000 to 11,000, and Korley's were 30,000.*

*On the ultrasound, they noticed her spleen was enlarged, and her kidneys were also like a set of horseshoes. At some point in my pregnancy, I had come into contact with something that caused her to have cancer of the blood, which we call leukemia. Those words were not on my radar at all. At this time, she was three months old.*

*Being in healthcare, I knew we were about to embark on this chemotherapy journey, and it was going to be very aggressive.*

*By the time she was six months old, she was swollen beyond recognition. They had her in a special bed to help her skin from falling apart. We basically lived in the hospital for three months. It was a terrible time.*

*The doctors pretty much said there's nothing else we can do. I begged the doctors not to give up on her, and I knew God had here in His hands.*

*The next day she passed a huge blood clot through her diaper, which was causing her to bleed so much because of the amounts of chemo she had been given. We experienced a huge turnaround after that. They took out her spline because she couldn't take a bottle because her mouth was so sore.*

*Finally, some good news came and by the time she was four-years-old, we were completely free from chemo.*

*From the age of four until nine, Korley lived a completely normal life.*

*She was nine years old when she came running down the basketball floor and we noticed her lips would turn blue, causing her to have to sit down. Since we were nearing her oncology appt, I decided to just talk with him at that appointment.*

*The doctor recommended we do some pulmonary tests to check her oxygen levels. They thought she might have asthma, so they gave her an inhaler, which didn't help a bit. While they were doing a biopsy of her lungs, the doctors made a horrible discovery. As my heart proceeded to collapse, he said, "these are the worst lungs I have ever seen in any human being ever." They believed it was due to the extensive amount of chemo she experienced as an infant.*

*Immediately they began plans for a lung transplant. She was going to need a bi-lateral lung transplant. In that time span, we went to Pittsburg twice for lung transplant evaluation. She was nine years old at that time.*

*Korley continued to decline rapidly, spending many days at Vanderbilt hospital. As her mom, I couldn't believe that I was watching my sweet little girl fight for her life once again.*

*For 30 days, she laid in a hospital bed waiting to get stronger so she could get her lungs in Pittsburg. We found out later that many times the lungs were approved for her, but she just wasn't strong enough to make the trip.*

*They began to press us for palliative care and to consider taking her off the breathing machine.*

*As a family, we chose not to take her off, but to allow God to stop her heart when He was ready for her.*

*God chose to stop her heart on February 2, 2011.*

As I interviewed Korey's mom (Becky Davis), I asked her a few questions I believe will be helpful to those on this journey and included her answers below.

### #1 How did your first month of grief feel like?

*I learned that no matter how many loving, supportive hands reached out to us, there are some paths you have to tread alone. Part of me died with Korley. I never blamed or was angry with God. I had days and days of loneliness, a period of unbelief, numbness, the need to know exactly where her spirit was; I asked God every day to tell her I loved her. People would say to me* how strong I was, which opened the door to give HIM all the credit. "In my weakness, He is strong."

#### #2 What was the greatest surprise in your grief process?
That there were hundreds of mothers who understood exactly how I felt, and they were not judgmental. I didn't have to bear this burden alone.

#### #3 What was the most difficult step in moving forward in your life?
I had to create a new normal. Cooking and getting out five plates, then remembering I needed only four now. Knowing what to do with her clothes was probably the hardest because I didn't want anybody to touch them.

#### #4 How do you handle holidays/birthdays?
Korey and I share the same birthday, which makes it double hard, but I chose to focus on the happy, wonderful, and good memories we shared together.

My family chooses to do the holidays in out of the ordinary ways. It seems to be less painful.

#### #5 What are some of the things you do to keep her memory alive?
We always encourage everyone to speak her name, recalling memories to us, always makes us as a family smile. We stay involved with Korey's friends. Her friends carried me through her "growing up period" of high school, graduation, college, etc. They included me, and I love them for that. Her friends come and eat with me on "our" birthday.

We named our goat farm after her, and when people ask what Halo K stands for, I'm happy to tell them Korey's story. The last thing we as a family honor with is "We Keep Living." Korey would want that!

Are you registered as an Organ Donor?

Organ donation is the process when a person allows an organ of their own to be removed and transplanted to another person, legally, either by consent while the donor is alive or dead with the assent of the next of kin. For more information: DONATELIFETN.org.

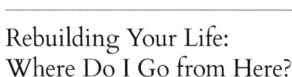

CHAPTER 13

# Rebuilding Your Life:
# Where Do I Go from Here?

This question finally comes to us all: "What do I do now?" and is compounded by another one, "Who am I now?"

Rebuilding your life does not mean you've abandoned or forgotten your loved one or that you no longer love him or her anymore. You don't have to choose between living again and remembering your loss.

It's time to give yourself permission to live again, to laugh again. To be present with those you love again. It's time to start living again-without feeling guilty.

Here's the bottom-line, friends: grieving is HARD, but before we can move forward, we must decide to change some things. Change is not a dirty word! It sometimes stretches us and makes us more awake to life.

Sometimes loving ourselves enough to change is something very foreign to us. We are great at taking care of all those around us, except us!

CHANGE will come, and it has to come to move forward!

It might occur in different ways sometimes. Some may be deliberate, some intentional, some may be slow to happen, and others might be overnight. All of the changes will help you gain clarity on the "new you."

Unfortunately, we all were not given a choice about whether we wanted to travel this journey or not. You have the power inside you on how well you will love yourself and embrace this new life.

Your success will be based on your attitude and perspective.

Anyone who knows me, knows I love butterflies. I love what Richard Bach wrote: "What the caterpillar calls the end of the world, the master calls a butterfly."

How will you look at your "New Life?" As a caterpillar or a butterfly?

Things that were helpful for me:

- Individual counseling
- Staying active with family and friends.
- Meditating 10-15 minutes every morning (Just being alone in silence became a sacred time for me).
- Stick positive "who I am" affirmations on my mirror (example: I am smart, I am courageous, I am loved, I am a good friend).
- Love yourself more. (Get massages, pedicures, etc.)
- Make a list of things that make you happy when you do them, such as movies, theaters, hiking, listening to music, etc.
- Engage in physical activity. Join a gym, try a yoga class, try new walking routes.
- Invest in a week or weekend retreat. This is something I chose to do for myself and I can say it was the best thing I ever did. A day spa or retreat can be a vital physical or mental experience to help you renew and rejuvenate your new life.
- Keep old traditions and make new ones. Many find comfort in family traditions. If you choose, keep practicing the traditions you love, but also try starting new ones. This will allow you to honor the past and move forward toward a new future.
- Every once in a while, stay in your PJs, watch movies and eat CHOCOLATE. It's OK!

Get Back in The Game. Life is a Gift and Happiness is FREE!!!!

CHAPTER **14**

# Pennies from Heaven— A Gift from Above

Going through the pain of losing a loved one, I now have a deeper appreciation for how precious life is and for how time can fly by without me ever taking notice. For how important it is to tell the people in your life how valuable they are to you and to thank God every day how blessed I am for the life He has given me.

## SHAWN'S STORY

*As long as I live, I will never forget the events that made up the first 21 days of June 2014. These days were filled with some of my greatest joys and, to date, my greatest heartache. As soon as the school year ended that May, I packed up and moved home to help my sisters and my mom take care of our dad. He had been diagnosed with a rare type of cancer, and the doctors had prepared us that the outlook was not good. In my mind, I could hear what the doctors were saying, but honestly, I never really allowed myself to go there because we were a family that loved and loved BIG, and if anyone could beat the odds, this gang could.*

*The next days were filled with "The Girls" (my two sisters, my momma, and myself) taking care of our hero around the clock. These days were filled with laughter, tears, sleepless nights, and some amazing "God Winks."*

*My dad and I have always been close, but during this time, our relationship grew in places in my heart I never knew existed. During these summer days together, my dad and I would talk about all kinds of things. The greatest blessing during these days was that my dad never lost his sense of humor and the ability to still, "Count it ALL joy!" Even when he knew his days on Earth were numbered, he still could find the strength to say, "Girls, I am not afraid to die; I KNOW I am headed to heaven, BUT I will miss y'all so much; our family is just so much fun!"*

*And this, for me, was where "Pennies from Heaven" became my lifeline to my dad. As tears rolled down my face, I ask my dad to please send us a sign that he was watching over his girls. He looked at me with these huge brown eyes and said, "I gotcha, girl. I will always send you pennies from Heaven."*

*And to this day, he does. My dad's wishes were to be cremated and his ashes spread in several different places. The "Girls" took a 1500-mile Joy Journey to spread our beloved dad's ashes. I will never forget our first set of pennies we found. We stopped to get gas in Birmingham, Al. As we pulled into the gas station, we could have chosen from about 40 different pumps. We finally found one that worked for us, and as I got out to pump the gas, on top of the tanks, there they were, pennies for all his girls.*

*Tears rolling down my face, I looked to Heaven and thanked both my fathers, my earthly and my heavenly for the beautiful reminder that even in death, you are always with me and that as Christians, I know without a shadow of a doubt in my mind that I will one day see those beautiful browns again, but until then I will keep collecting all the pennies from Heaven that I can find.*

**Pennies from Heaven for us all**

I don't pretend to understand the meaning of finding pennies on the ground or any other place until it happened to me.

I had decided to go to Gatlinburg for a long weekend to work on this book. Nestled in the mountains is the cutest little cabin I love to stay in when I'm writing. After I unpacked the car, I started looking for a desk or table to set my computer on. There wasn't a desk, but there was a small side table that could serve as a computer table. On top of the desk were an old jam box, a lamp, and a box of tissues.

My lucky day, it was perfect! I proceeded to pick up the jam box, and what do you think was under it? Yep! Two pennies, one was dull, and the other was bright and shiny. Tears immediately began to flow down my cheeks. I felt it was my first sign from above that Jim was alright, and he wanted me to be alright. I felt God was saying that this old, dull penny represented my past life with Jim, and this new shiny penny represented my new life that was now emerging.

After that experience, pennies began to flow from Heaven. I was beginning to get so many pennies that I got a little jar and wrote "Pennies from Heaven" on the outside of it.

Do I really know where those pennies came from? Of course not, but I choose to believe that God and my special angel are watching over me because every time I see a penny on the ground, the most overwhelming sense of peace comes over me. The kind of peace that comforts me. The kind of peace that only comes from God.

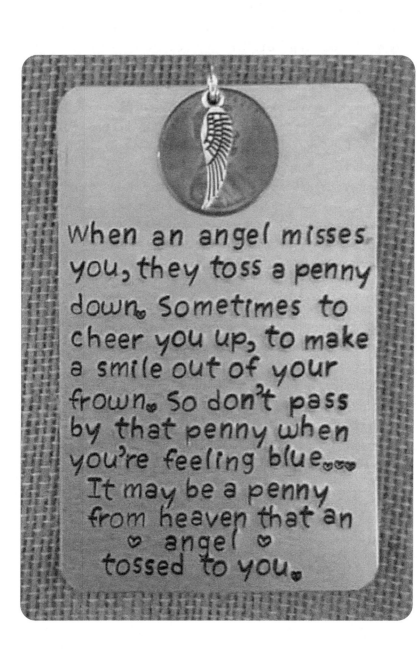

When an angel misses you, they toss a penny down. Sometimes to cheer you up, to make a smile out of your frown. So don't pass by that penny when you're feeling blue... It may be a penny from heaven that an ♡ angel ♡ tossed to you.

# Conclusion—What to Do Now

Embrace the peace of God!

The believer who places his or her confidence in a loving God and is thankful in every circumstance will possess a supernatural peace. An inner calm will dominate the heart. The faithful believer will know peace, with his heart and mind are "guarded" by it, despite the tempest raging without. No one, especially those outside Christ, will be able to fathom that peace. To most, it will remain a mystery how someone can be so serene in the midst of turmoil.

The peace that comes from being in a right relationship with God is not the peace of the world. The world's peace depends on having favorable circumstances: if things are going well, then we feel peaceful; when things go awry, the peace quickly dissipates.

I'm so glad that I know that peace, and I hope you have experienced it too. Whether we believe it or not, God has been with us throughout our lives and is with us this very minute. See www.gotquestions.org for more.

# Resources

*GotQuestions.org*

*National Suicide Prevention Line: 1-800-273-8255*

*Reflections of a Grieving Spouse* by H. Norman Wright

*Experiencing Grief* by Kenneth Haugk

# About the Author

Cherie Jobe is a speaker, author, life coach and a retired hairdresser of 40 years. Her friendly smile, honest transparency, and genuine love for people-along with her Tennessee twang-endear her to audiences wherever she goes. Having encountered heartache, pain, and rejection Cherie understands the trials of "real life". She speaks to thousands each year, encouraging, equipping, and empowering women to live out who they were "designed" to be. Cherie lives outside Nashville, Tennessee.

# Acknowledgments

It takes a festival of family and friends to pull off a book project such as this. Many of you have walked every step of this journey with me. Maybe it came through an encouraging word, helping me pray for direction, or possibly crying a bucket of tears with me. I will forever be thankful for you!

My husband of 16 years: Jim Jobe. I was so blessed with a husband like you who enhanced, encouraged, and enriched my life. You taught me how to live life to the fullest, as well as how to embrace death in the end.

On the front of this book is the last beach trip we took; we always loved to watch the sunsets together. I'm positive that, in heaven, you're experiencing the most brilliant ones ever!

My ministry advisory team: Karen Thrasher, Sherri Rambo, Chandra Porter, Patsy Highland—thankful for all your support over the years!

My special prayer partners: Terry and Joanne Theis

My weekly tribal friends: Connie Huddleston, Donna Stearns, Suzanne Moss—life is always better when traveled with friends!

My new friend and book designer/editor: Andy Garrison—I will forever be grateful to you for your patience and desire to make this special project exactly what it was "Designed" to be...to give people HOPE to live again!

To all those who shared their "without" stories. Those who live daily with a broken heart, but have chosen to keep moving forward with their lives.

My Savior Jesus Christ, who walks beside me everyday reminding me I am NEVER alone. Deuteronomy 31:6

# Other Books By Cherie Jobe:

SECRETS FROM BEHIND THE CHAIR

Through a series of heartrending secrets, Cherie Jobe offers
the gifts of hope and wisdom, teaching how to be content,
peaceful, and strong, even during the bad hair days of life.

SURVIVING BAD HAIR DAYS

A series of stories about Cherie's and others' bad hair days and how
they dealt with them. It offers genuine friendship, candid humor and
wise counseling as clients, friends and acquaintances share childhood
nightmares, relationship struggles and deeply hidden hurts.

## New Beginnings

Cherie Jobe hosts a women's conference every February.
More than 700 women have attended. For more information
about the event, visit www.CherieJobe.com.